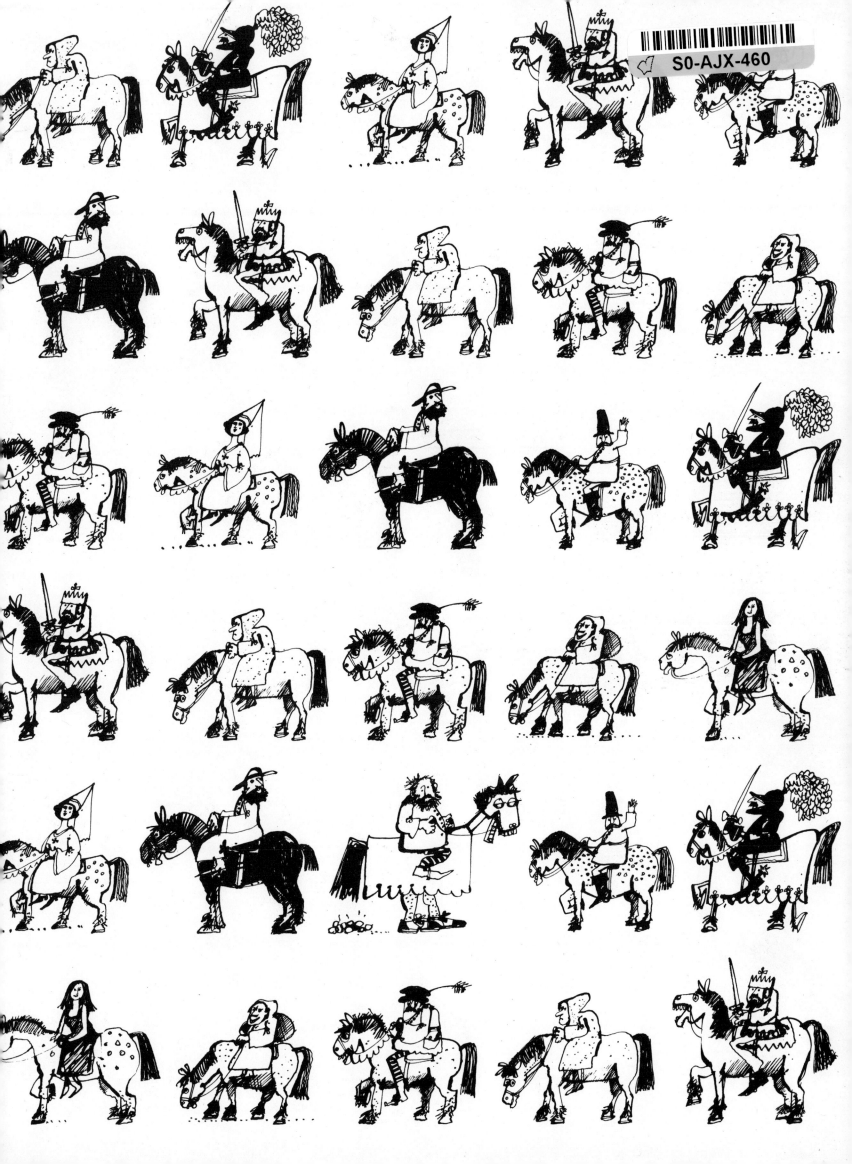

GRAHAM CLARKE'S
HISTORY OF ENGLAND

All Good Wishes

from

Graham Clarke

14 Nov. 87

Graham Clarke's History of England

Phaidon · Oxford

For Grandpa Ray,
who for our delight turned the
minor sin of exaggeration into
a major art form

Author's Note

I should like to thank Roger Sears of Phaidon Press, who told me I'd got to write a History Book, and Marie Leahy, my editor, who made sure I did.

My thanks, too, to Barbara Mercer, Phaidon's designer, and to Tony Smith, typographer, who carried out the design and incorporated my own typeface 'Wartsand Hall'.

The colour plates are reproduced from Graham Clarke's *History of England* prints. The original etchings are printed from copper plates on hand-made paper supplied by Barcham Green and Company. They are coloured by hand and presented in two editions: Edition A, consisting of 200 individual copies, signed and numbered; and a Portfolio Edition, consisting of 200 portfolio sets containing all eighteen images and accompanying *Notes for the Interested*. The series is presented in three parts: Ye Firste, Ye Seconde and Ye Thyrde. Edition A and the Portfolio Edition were jointly published during 1986 and 1987 by the artist, Christie's Contemporary Art, and Alex Gerrard Fine Art.

Phaidon Press Limited, Littlegate House, St Ebbe's Street, Oxford OX1 1SQ

First published 1987
© Phaidon Press Limited 1987

British Library Cataloguing in Publication Data

Clarke, Graham,
    Graham Clarke's History of England.
    I. Title
    828'.91407   PN6175

    ISBN 0–7148–2464–X

Typeset in Wartsand Hall © Graham Clarke by Universe Typesetters Limited and Bembo by Facet (London) Limited

Printed in England by The Roundwood Press, Kineton, Warwickshire

CONTENTS

FOREWORD

A large welcoming advertisement at Heathrow Airport reads: 'The past can only be cloned. The future must be created.'

In this absorbing series of pictures and notes, including notes on notes, Graham Clarke proves that history can be created too. He sticks to a chronological arrangement, if reluctantly, and finds fun at every point in time to which he turns. The Revd. T. 'Pongo' Pigtrinket-Smith's alternative version, to which he refers in his preface, is eagerly awaited. These are obviously not the last pictures or words.

Nor are they the first. Back in the nineteenth century John Leech illustrated Gilbert à Beckett's *The Comic History of England*, serving up in as 'palatable a shape as he could the facts of English history'. That was the work of a partnership, as was *1066 and All That*. Mr Clarke, however, who is as interested in evidence as in facts (a sign of the times and of the revolution in historical scholarship), works on his own.

The reason why I started this Foreword with Heathrow Airport is that I first saw the illustrations in this volume at an exhibition at the other airport, Gatwick. I left on a long journey by air both stimulated and refreshed. I am sure people who buy this book will feel the same.

ASA BRIGGS

Worcester College, Oxford
28 May 1987

PREFACE

Nearly all books on this subject seem to begin with a phrase such as 'But why another book on the History of England?' So does mine.

'But why another book on the History of England?'

Until a few years ago I was under the impression that my etchings were completely self-explanatory and that the average person had only to look at one for a couple of seconds and the very meaning of life itself would instantly become clear. Apparently I was wrong. I was therefore obliged to jot down a sentence or two as 'Notes for the Interested' in order that the more serious student of my work might grasp its full significance.

The fact that a 'bit of writing' was necessary became even more obvious when I began work on the History of England series of prints here presented. Vast areas of total ignorance were revealed in the course of conversations with my publishers, customers, colleagues and especially with our dog and David Case of Christie's Contemporary Art. So the immense task of research and writing began – but with a certain amount of caution, as it is well known that too much factual knowledge on a given subject is liable to cramp style and hide the truth. Better to trust to intuition, common sense and an understanding of human nature than do too much mugging up when dealing with an important subject like English History.

It is therefore with a certain amount of reluctance that I have agreed to arrange this book in chronological order, thus following nearly all previous works on the subject. This was done merely to please Phaidon Press, my publishers, people of the utmost charm but little expertise in these affairs. The far more exciting anachronological approach was of course the one used by the Rev. T. 'Pongo' Pigtrinket-Smith in his now highly regarded archaeological works, during which he buried Roman coins all over Wiltshire. (His book *Smashing Old Vases* is still the standard work on the subject.) To him I owe a great debt of gratitude for scrupulously checking all the dates referred to in this volume.

I am deeply grateful, too, to Dame Cecily Thripp, D.D.T., for her kind encouragement, tireless research, and occasional loan of her automatic pencil-sharpener.

Most of all, however, I must thank my esteemed colleague Professor A. Ristotle-Bogwicket, V.S.O.P. Without the generous loan of his unique and priceless collection of archival material and 'related artefacts' the preparation of this book would simply not have been possible.

G. C.

Boughton Monchelsea
9.41 a.m. Monday, 16th Feb. 1987

1 DUNROAMIN'

The Moon
(circa 2000 BC)

Until about 2000 BC we English hadn't taken much interest in History. We were quietly having our Bronze Age[1] – and a pretty good one it was too: we wore fur coats from Monday to Friday and smart blue paint at weekends. We were more than happy to leave Real History to the Hebrews, Egyptians, Greeks, etc., all of whom were quite good at it in their various ways – especially the Hebrews, who although not very numerous were particularly well documented. The Egyptians on the other hand were good at building things but hardly bothered about their writing, while the Greeks quite frankly were a bit on the 'intellectual' side for most people's taste and enjoyed making statues without arms when they weren't merely thinking.

However, just after midnight on 31 December 2001 BC a load of Celts suddenly arrived and announced that the Iron Age had begun. Their vicars were called Druids and they wore long cloaks and pointed hats and organized festivals all day long. Quite understandably they were keen to get History off the ground in their newly adopted country and consequently decided to build a stonehenge.

Until recently we have only been able to guess at the precise function of this ancient structure and it must be said that some of my fellow historians have trotted out some pretty far-fetched theories. Dame Cecily Thripp D.D.T., for example, is convinced that it was a prehistoric swimming-pool. This idea, though, simply does not hold water.

However, a recently discovered document does throw new light on the subject. It is translated for us here from the original Bronze Age by my esteemed colleague Professor A. Ristotle Bogwicket G.W.R., recently Senior Tutor in Pre-Skifflite Studies at the University of Barking-up-the-Creek.

Mrs Elsie Trewergle,
Hut 4, Chysauster, Cornwall

Dear Mum,

This is the worst site I've ever been on. The wind blows across this bit of Wiltshire something chronic. Not just the wind, either, but rain and sleet too, just like the end of the Ice Age that Gran used to go on about.

These Druids are real weirdos, Mum, wandering about in a dream all the time and chatting about the phases of the moon and such. They still don't seem to have decided exactly what it is that we are supposed to be building. A sort of Cosmic Calculator someone said – whatever that's supposed to be.

What's upset us most, though, is the size of the stones. They're gigantic. I mean *really* big. Jones 'the stones', the delivery bloke from Cadwallader & Cadwallader, says it's cheaper like that. It's all right for him: what about us poor nurks who've got to cut them up into nice neat little bricks?

If things don't improve soon I can see we'll all be walking off this job and then where will they be? I'll tell you: the thing won't get built at all and they'll be left with a circle of damn great rocks and nothing to do with them.

So I might be back home a bit sooner than we thought, eh?

Love to all at Number 4.

Yours,

With the benefit of hindsight we may venture to surmise that he was not mistaken.

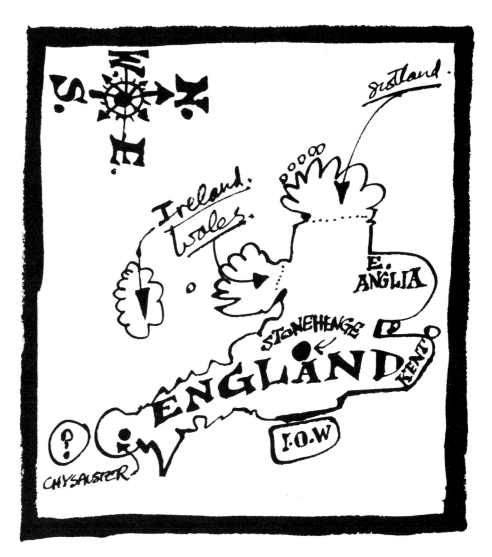

1. Opinions differ as to the origin of the terms 'Iron Age' and 'Bronze Age'. Some historians believe that as iron objects were made in the Iron Age and bronze objects in the Bronze Age there may be some connection. (Would that it were so simple, say I. What are we then to deduce about Cabbage, Luggage, Slippage – let alone Roughage?)

1 DUNROAMIN'

II ROMANS DO

Haggis Warrior
(circa 250 A.D.)

To L.P. Grimbald Esq.,
Messrs. Grimbald & Lugworth (Light Removals) Ltd.,
1, Watling Street,
Dover, Kent

Dear Grimbald partner and old friend,
What must you think of me? Neither hide nor hair of me for nigh on two months. I expect you'd begun to think I'd run off with old Dobbin and the firm's best waggon. The fact is that I'd no sooner dropped off that barrel of mead at *The Jolly Sailor* when tramping round the corner comes a bunch of those legionary chaps, all trendy leather and fancy metalwork. 'Here my man' one of them shouts, 'Hadrian's Wall, and fast.' And with that they all leaped up behind me into the waggon. Quite startled poor Dob – not to mention me. 'Scuse me' says I, as polite as you like, 'but I ain't adoin' no Adrians Wall today. I've a load of woad for the Isle of Thanet and then a crate of sickles for the Boadicea Waggon Works at Venta Icenorum.

To cut a long story short – or, rather, to stop me being cut short – I eventually agreed to collect their clobber from the *Mediterranean Prawn*, their galley. So with the ten bods, ten spare suits of armour, and God knows how much vino, hair oil and spaghetti, we set off up Watling Street.

Well it's not going to surprise you to hear that after a couple of leagues the front axle went. It's been on the blink for months, as you well know. There was this grinding crash and an almighty bump and Dobbin came to a dead halt. 'Well that lets me off the hook' I thought, rather pleased. 'Steering's gone, gents' says I. 'Too much weight up front, just like I told you. It'll take at least two weeks to fix that. You'd best find yourselves alternative transport.'

'You just carry on, old man' they says. 'Don't you worry about your miserable cart.'

'But it won't steer, gents. It won't turn no corners.'

'You just trot on, steering or no steering, or you and your odiferous quadruped are liable to end up as a lion's breakfast at the Colosseum.'

So I did, straight across field, farmyards, cabbage, cattle, molehill and mountain: straight as an arrow – as much out of cussedness as cowardice, I'm pleased to say. Anyway, old Dob has more or less recovered and the waggon will soon be back in working order so I'll be on my way back down South again just as soon as I can.

Please tell the wife.

Yours, etc.

At the time of writing his letter Wulfric Lugworth was of course quite unaware of the consequences of his unorthodox style of navigation. It was only on his return journey that he realized that the ten soldiers that he had been obliged to transport were merely the advance party for a further 80,000 troops, required to quell a minor uprising of the much-dreaded Haggi tribe.[1] Being strangers to these parts (and good army men too) they simply 'followed the lot in front' and went trampling with their 160,000 feet over everything that lay in their path.

Bringing up the rear was a small but highly important company of generals and bigshots. They found the straight road idea 'terribly smart' and, indeed, were so impressed that soon it became more or less 'de rigueur' throughout the entire Roman Empire.

In the opinion of Dr Lucas Thurkettle G.B.H., author of *Hengist the Horsa and Other Works on Early English Transport*, 'Never has one humble man had such a profound and long-lasting effect upon a ruling nation – or stolen so much Campari while doing it.'

Who are we to argue?

1. Much has been written on the subject of this particularly belligerent race. Their weaponry is thought to have been unique and no other tribe has since sought to imitate it. The most devastating and, it must be said, cruel weapon used by these wild men was the 'Haggi' (from which their name derived).

Haggis consisted of a light skin bag stuffed with a mixture of unmentionable substances which was either flung or kicked into the air to land amongst unsuspecting (and very fastidious) Roman soldiers. The effect was reinforced by the use of a second, sonic weapon which emitted a high-pitched screeching sound that caused the Roman ranks to drop their weapons and clap their hands over their ears. It was known as the 'bag of pipes'.

II ROMANS DO

During his scholarly researches into the Alfredian Cake Heresy in the famous library of St Inkers College, the distinguished historian Professor A. Ristotle Bogwicket L.M.S. was fortunate enough to discover a remarkable document concerning our national hero King Arthur. Most of our notions concerning Arthur are based on works written centuries after his death by such worthies as Mallory, Spencer, Dryden, Tennyson, Thripp, etc., and so can hardly be considered reliable. Some records originate from France: they cannot be taken seriously, for obvious reasons.

In the light of this new evidence our conception of Arthur as a dignified, heroic warrior-king leading his courtly knights to deeds of great bravery must now (I regret to say) be somewhat modified.

The Arthur Diaries
(Extracts February 516 to May 517 AD)

FEB 1. Tournament. Mercia v Wessex Round Table. Rain stopped play 4.30p.m. Six injured, no dead. Man of the match (wouldn't you know it) Sir Gawain, with 9.7 points.

FEB 8. Tournament. Veterans All Europe Team Match (Charity Do). Winners, St George's Red Cross Team. Ten injured, two dead.

FEB 15. Queen off with Launcelot again. He's welcome, silly old fool. Just hope he's up to it

FEB 17. Measured up for new suit of armour. Inside leg same as last time, waist a bit larger. Looking for something lightweight, something a bit summery – ceremonial only, of course.

FEB 20. Yet another tournament. This time Winchester Chamber of Commerce All Comers Invitation. Winner, St Michael of the High Street. All injured, Sir Winfield fatally.

DRAGON (Adult Male.)

FEB 27. My birthday. Useless presents from all concerned – again. Rain.

MAY 8. Hot weather. Lightweight armour still not ready.

SEPT 24. New armour too bleddy tight. Decided to teach armourer a lesson and stick him in the stocks for a bit. 'But I've got an urgent alteration job to do for that nice Mr Gawain' he protests. Gawain, Gawain, that's all I hear nowadays.

OCT 6. Sent Gawain off to look for Holy Grail. Do him good.

OCT 7. Tournament. Away to Northumbria. Lost 6-4. Rain.

OCT 8. Reports of dragons again. What's wrong with people nowadays? Sent Sir 'charm your pants off' Launcelot to sort it out once and for all. Came back with another princess. God knows where they all come from. Looks more like the barmaid at The Ratskinners Arms to me.

OCT 9. Gawain back. Says he can't find it. He's not likely to, I keep it wrapped up in an old vest on top of my wardrobe. 'Her Ladyship' says we must have Mr and Mrs Gawain round to dinner some time. Not if I can help it.

OCT 10. Dinner party. Venison again. Drank too much as usual, only thing to do.

OCT 11. Headache. Rain.

OCT 15. Went to collect new sword, Ex Calibre, bleddy great thing. Couldn't hardly lift it off the ground. Good job it's only for show.

OCT 20. Tournament. 'Newts' of the Round Table v. Chevaliers de France. Utter farce as usual. Newts 10 Chevs. de France 0. Can't see why they keep coming over. To show off their fancy outfits to the ladies, I suppose. Bleddy Launcelot at it again. He's the fourth one this week.

NOV 1. Union of Candlemakers & General Lamplighters on strike. Talk about the

Dark Ages, it's always the same this time of the year. Merlin ought to invent electric light instead of boiling up toads, the silly old celt.

DEC 24. New armour comes back from re-fit. Still too tight. Decide to order new suit. Choose a rather dashing silver 28-piece from pattern book.

DEC 25. Christmas Day. Can't get plumber. Unblock drains myself. Sir Galahad waltzes in wearing identical suit. 'Go off and search for Holy Grail' I say. 'I might have a little look for it later' he says, winking at 'Her Ladyship'. Bleddy cheek.

FEB 27. Birthday. My turn to pay for party as usual. Lady of Shallott 'throws wobbler' as usual. Galahad at it, venison fork-resistant, I drank too much – all as usual.

FEB 28. Headache. Birthday Honours Knight Dubbing all morning. Ex Calibre too bleddy heavy if you ask me.

MAR. 13. (Friday) Launcelot comes round. Can he borrow horse as his is in for 10,000 mile service. Takes my best and crashes into oak tree on way home from Temperance Meeting at Ratskinners Arms.

MAR. 16. New armour ready at last. Paid armourer, including 35 per cent rustproofing surcharge. Bit tight below chest.

MAR. 20. Rain. Signs of rust round rivets,

MAR. 25. Merlin suggests digging tunnel to France. Most stupid of his stupid ideas yet. 'I dare say Guinivere and the Chevaliers de France think it's a good idea,' say I, 'but I don't.' He slouches off to his shed.

MAR. 26. Mixed Veg. soup tastes a bit funny. Decide to reinstate royal food-taster as soon as poss.

MAR. 27. Buried new food-taster next to the others.

APRIL 1. 'Huge great army of Vikings landed in Anglia!' announces Galahad. Have mild heart-attack trying to get into second-best suit of armour. Assemble approx. 800 horsemen and 5,000 foot soldiers. Agree terms. Her Ladyship not about. Probably at hairdresser's. Visit privy yet again. Come out and Galahad shouts 'April Fool!' Everyone laughs heartily (except me). I start to imagine how much taller Sir G. might be after a couple of weeks on the rack. Just my luck that the Incarcerators and Master Torturers are out on strike – 'unsocial working conditions'.

APRIL 5. Can't seem to get anyone interested in my scheme for a Horse Droppings Marketing Board. Best idea anyone's had around these parts for ages. 'You could call it The Equestrian Refuse Directorate' says smart alec Galahad. No doubt he thinks it's funny.

APRIL 24. Rain.

MAY 8. First day back from rather damp two weeks in Lyonesse and what do I find? Yet another union has been formed while I was on my hols – The Amalgamated Society of Grail Hunters, Dragon Slayers and General Quest Operatives – and they want more money. So much for chivalry. Who'd be a king in this day and age? I ask you.

MAY 9. Rain.

A Holy Grail of the type frequently mislaid during Arthurian Times.

The complete version of *The Arthur Diaries* is to be published by Fungal & Peabody in 520 weekly instalments.

III DARTHUR.

IV HASTINGS JOB

Coming to terms with The Battle of Hastings has always represented something of a problem for us English. We are not in the habit of losing battles, particularly to 'persons from across the English channel'. It may, though, be helpful to remember that the Normans and their king, William, were not frenchmen. They were only accidentally living in france and quite understandably would have preferred to live in England.

Edward the Confessor[1] had more or less promised the throne of England to William the Norman of Norman Normandy but unfortunately had not mentioned it to his proper successor King Harold. So the poor man was completely taken by surprise and was obliged to use the services of untrained men – with highly unfortunate opthalmic consequences.

For the last 920 years the legend that Harold was shot in the eye by a stray Norman Arrow has remained unquestioned. However, in the course of his diligent research into this particular aspect of the events of 1066 my colleague Prof. A. Ristotle Bogwicket v.s.o.p. of St Aggers College, Bognor Regis, came across the following letter which hints at a new and much more plausible theory.

Dear Mum,
Something really strange happened this morning. We'd just arrived at Hastings and were unpacking our fishing rods and thinking about having a swift half in the 'Jolly Sailor' when a posh-looking bloke trots up on a great big horse.

'You're conscripted' he says. 'You're in King Harold's Army.'

'Not so, Guvnor' we say. 'We are the Mid-Wessex Angling Society Annual Outing.'

'Come on now chaps', he says. 'Be brave and decent fellows. We're short of good fighting men. It's an honour to serve one's King and Country.'

'I'll tell you what we'll do,' says Egbert,

'You get your Harold to present the prizes at our Ladies' Night next month and we'll have a go at those french chaps for you. It'll be a laugh, won't it lads?'

'Well, I'll do my best', he says.

'Righto then, Squire', says our Egbert. 'Here's four good men and true, forsooth egad and all that. Lead on Macduff. Just show us those tiresome garlic guzzlers and we'll cut them up for bait. How many of them are there? Six? Seven?'

'About six thousand' says he, 'and they're not really french, they're Normans – well, Vikings, actually.'

'Vikings' squeaks Egbert, going all wobbly. 'Six thousand Vikings! Bye bye Guv.'

And that was the last we saw of him. Didn't even bother to pick up his new rod, did he? So they've given me a huge bow and arrow. I told them I'd never shot one in my life and wouldn't be able to hit a barn door at three paces with my eye sight. But they wouldn't listen.

'Great big chap like you?' they said. 'Just what we need – in fact you can be King Harold's bodyguard. You can stand just behind him and keep an eye on him.'

Wish us all luck for tomorrow, Mum.
Yours in Haste(ings)

Despite the rather erratic spelling and somewhat esoteric narrative-style of the foregoing, the information it provides points almost incontrovertibly to the fact that poor Harold had his eye poked out at the very moment when he turned round in his saddle to encourage his men. One of the worst own goals in History. The only conflicting evidence to this theory, apart from History Books, is the Bayeux Tapestry – and who's going to trust that load of french knitting?

Fig. 1

The so-called 'Bayeux'[2] tapestry is of course only one of several thousand such articles made in this Norman industrial centre.

The tapestry industry was of course in full swing long before William landed in Sussex and it would have been obvious to take along Queen Matilda and her squad of Norman Knitting Novices to record the event for the folks back home. The somewhat hasty style of the work and the positively skimpy lack of background detail are indicative of the speed at which the whole piece was dashed off.

It is most important to realize that tapestries were not stuck up on the wall in one long piece as the so called 'Bayeux' is presented today. We now know that they were viewed as one continuous programme passing from one roller to another across a hole cut in the front of a specially designed wooden box (see Fig. 1).

The poorer classes might well see such things when they were set up at fairs or markets, where they would be charged a small sum to peruse the latest battle or adventure programme. Most folk had their own 'boîte à vue', sometimes quite an elaborate affair with an intricate system of pulleys and handles to operate the rollers at an aesthetically acceptable speed. These were sometimes powered by wind or water, or even by a dog or petty criminal in a treadwheel. The tapestry might thus be seen from end to end without involving any effort on the part of the viewer.

A predictable result of the enormous popularity of the medium was that some people would spend several hours a day merely watching tapestry, even though some of the programmes, it was thought, contained too much violence or scenes of too explicit a nature to be suitable for young people or those of a nervous disposition. Tapestries gradually became more commercial and some even carried a certain amount of advertising material, usually along the borders. For instance, the rather curious creatures depicted along the length of the 'Bayeux' almost certainly represent items on the menu of a chain of Norman fast-food restaurants. (The fact that such creatures are now extinct indicates yet again the capacity of the french to eat strange objects in vast quantities.)

It is believed by many scholars that the popularity of tapestry had many highly undesirable repercussions, including the Black Death of 1348, Moslems, warts and people with ginger hair and pointed shoes; also a general lack of respect for authority amongst the young.

1. No doubt a very decent man in his way, although exactly what it was he'd done wrong that merited so much confession is lost in the mists of time. A pity.
2. The original name of the town has long been forgotten as it only took on the name Bayer-yeux (later Bayeux) late in the eleventh century, presumably as a result of Harold's nasty accident.

Harraps French/English Dictionary (New Shorter)
Bayer bajē : To stand gaping. To gape at the moon.
Yeux : eyes

IV HASTINGS JOB

V KEEP YOUR SAXON

Lady Godiva
(in Civvies)

No sooner had William the Conqueror snatched the Crown of England from our poor dead Harold, scratched it with his penknife to see if it was real gold and tried it on for size than he began to wonder what the rest of his ill-gotten gains might be worth.

There is no more positive proof – if proof were needed – of William's true nature than that massive Tax Collectors' Beano recorded for posterity in the Domesday Book. Money, money, money, that was all he was interested in, and no sooner had he moved into his newly purloined castle than he summoned his civil servants and shouted:

'Allez-vous out there à la doublay and

trouvez damn vite what this lot's worth.'

So off they trotted, all over England, snooping about with clipboards and binoculars and jotting down notes on how much land there was for pasture, how many manor houses, churches, pigsties, privvies – in fact anything he could clap a tax on or turn into ready cash.

As might be expected, petty bureaucrats were as idle then as they are now and since William was in a hurry, and as he could never check the facts anyway, they invented most of the details. After all, it was easy enough to count 3 french hens or even 12 oxen, but who was going to check 80,000 eels or hang around counting bumble bees? In fact, by the time they were getting to the

24

end of the job they were making up entire villages just to get it finished. (Which incidentally explains why it has been impossible to trace so many of the places recorded in the Book.)

The accuracy of the listings has rarely been challenged, though my learned colleague A. Ristotle-Bogwicket G.B.H., finder of The Missing Pages (see below) has suggested that the Rufus Spratling Chronicle (see Chaper VI) may in fact be a more faithful record.

There was, however, another altogether more sinister reason for the compiling of the Domesday Book. It was part of a plan which, if it had succeeded, would have changed the course of History. The plan was to present England as a fully Normanized domaine and not as the Noble Land of King Alfred the Great and Fish and Chips. To this end whole areas of English life were deliberately excluded. Where, for example, are references to Real Ale Breweries? Roast Beef, Pancake Racing, or Morris Dancing with Lady Godiva, King Arthur and Cadbury's Chocolate?

The Domesday Book has coloured the views of historians for the last 900 years and it would no doubt have continued to do so but for the remarkable and fortuitous discovery by Professor A. Ristotle-Bogwicket of dozens of pages edited out of the original findings of King William's clipboard creepers. The evidence it provides is so controversial that, to avoid embarrassment, Professor Bogwicket has asked me not to mention the names of his rival scholars, in particular Dr Herbert Pune B.O.A.C., Dame Cecily Thripp D.D.T., and Mr David Case C.C.A., in whose wastepaper basket the missing pages were actually found.

The following extract concerning a small English village is no doubt typical of those entries which were 'edited out' at a very early stage.

Atte Bocton Monchensey in Ye Countie of Kente:

Ten arpents of beech woodlands
697 Ferrets 136 bull dogs 1 woodlouse
One Real Ale Brewery and eight nice pubs. Highly recommended Ye Albion Inne. (Morris dancing alternate Thursdays.)
Decente village greene set about with Conker Trees.
A Matche of Crykette with fyne performances by bothe the village blacksmith (batter) and ye Godiva Streakerlaydie.

Teatime score at ye Crykette:
Wessex and Anglia all out for 32
Bocton Monchensey 835 for 3

V KEEP YOUR SAXON

VI THE RUFUS SPRATLING CHRONICLE

The pyramidal structure of the Feudal System was conceived, put into practice and maintained rather more for the benefit of those in authority than for the well-being and happiness of the little peasant at the bottom of the pile.

The basic idea seems to have been that all poor people should work very hard every single day of their lives on land stolen from them by their Lord of the Manor, and that he in return should take their crops, cattle, prettier daughters and heads off more or less as he pleased.

The drawbacks of such an arrangement for the average serf are fairly obvious to the modern reader but before passing judgement we would do well to consider the evidence of the following document. Found in the cleaning lady's bucket-cupboard at the Royal College of Trainspotting, it challenges us to reject all our preconceptions and consider the facts anew.

Ye Breakfast Carp

My nayme is Rufus Spratling. I am part of the Feudal System. This is my Chronicle. I belonge to Baron L'Ardydah Philtheriche de Philtheriche. I am called Rufus after oure greate and goode King of that sayme nayme and Spratling after a close friend of my mother's.

Todaye it is my birthdaye. I believe I am about fourtye yeares olde. I had a lie in until nearlye 5 a.m. My Lord, who to me is always especially kind and generous, alloweth me to carry his breakfaste carp and giveth me a severe buffett about my eares as a birthdaye surprise.

My Lord was so impressed with the bean croppe from mine owne lyttel plotte that he generously tooketh ye lotte.

My Lord's Archery Practice. This tyme I was allowed to catch the arrow on a lyttel wooden shield, not in my hatte. O lucky fellow!

O foolish varlet that I am. I had to be put in the stocks for whistling at my work. 'Butte I am a happy man' I telleth my Lord. 'Well don't be' he sayeth. 'Thou hast no right.'

Beautiful cold, damp November. Was allowed to carry great stones as it was a holiday.

Fortune smileth upon me. I have been appointed to clean out castle draynes! 'How long hast thou worked here?' asketh my Lord.

'32 joyous years,' sayeth I. 'Since I was eight.'

'And how wouldst thou like to own thine very own wheelbarrow?' he asketh.

'Greatly, my Lord' sayeth I. 'In truth it is my one true ambition, if it please thee.'

'No, it does not please me and you can't' he sayeth wisely.

My Lord's brother ye Abbotte was good enough to accept double the usual tithe from my oat croppe, thus reducing my chances of goinge to Hell when I dye. Oh wise and holy man that he is.

While unblocking draynes was allowed to visit my wicked brother Egbold in my Lord's dungeoune as it is the tenth anniversary of his stealing my Lord's turnip. Left him in goode spirits consideringe...

My Lord letteth me cutte ye thistles, nettles and brambles around ye moate. He sayeth I may keep all I wishe for mine own purposes. In addition, he decreeth that all rain that falleth on our hutte roofs or plottes of land during the last week of Februarye we may keep for oure own purposes.

I requesteth a kind audience with my Lord to discuss a matter of verye greate importance to me.

'What is your name, twerp?' he sayeth.

'No, Rufus Spratling, my Lord. Rufus after our great and good king...'

'Get lost, foole. I'm busy' he kindly sayeth. 'Come back in five years.'

'Thank you greatly, my Lord' sayeth I.

· · ·

Archery practice. No shield this time but was allowed to run as fast as I wished. This in preparation for my Lord's Summer Holidaye. Great Excitement. I am to carry my Lord's second-best chain mail and all his horse's fodder for several hundred miles. It will be the firste time I have ventured beyond our village boundaries. 'You may come as a special treat' sayeth my Lord 'but will need to work nights to catch up if you are not killed.' 'Thank you, my Lord' sayeth I.

· · ·

Am home again and recovering well from plague and sundrie wounds.

· · ·

It is Christmas Daye and my Lord kindly decreeth that I might choppe logges for him all day, and all night too if I so wish. He wisely points out that this waye I shalle keepe warm. This I do, and enjoy sounds of merriment coming from within the castle walls. This remindeth me, and I request the honour of another audience with my Lord.

'Well, what is it this time, dolt?' he enquireth.

'I wish to marry a lady' say I.

'And who' he asketh 'is the lucky woman?'

'I have notte looked yette' sayeth I, 'for I did not have Your Lordship's permission.'

'Quite right too, muttonhead, and no you can't marry. I am too busy.'

'Thank you my Lord' sayeth I, 'but if it please your Lordship my name is notte Muttonhead. It is Rufus Spratling. Rufus after our...'

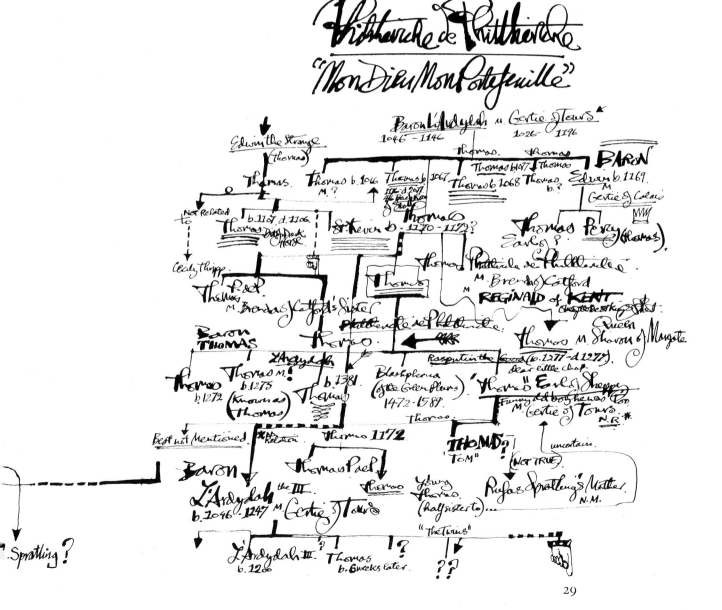

VI THE RUFUS SPRATLING CHRONICLE

VII JOLLY GOOD ROBIN HOOD

His Dad

The Printers Mark & Captons father

Sheriff of Nottingham

Ye Barmaid Marionne

As we know, Robin Hood combined the qualities of Morality, Illegality, Humour, Courage and general Snook-Cocking in such highly satisfactory proportions that he was and still is a truly popular hero.

In fact, much more is known about Robin Hood than we have been led to believe. Whilst carrying out his researches into early fifteenth-century printing techniques – and in particular the exquisite turnip-cuts of J. Caxton, father of the even more famous William of identical surname – my eminent fellow historian Professor A. Ristotle-Bogwicket was privileged to unearth and subsequently study what must surely be one of the rarest of all literary and historical treasures:

Ye Trew Storie and Funny Poemms of Robin Hoode and his Merrie Menne As Wrytten Bye Ye Said Robbyne Hode with Introductionne and Spellinge by Rev. F. Tuckke D.D.

Despite this rather lengthy title the book itself is what cognoscenti refer to as a rather slim volume and this, the Professor suggests, could well be why it has been passed by so many times on the shelves of one of our Great British Libraries. As far as we are able to ascertain there is only one copy in existence and it is our belief that upon publication in 1460 it was immediately suppressed, for although Hood himself had been dead for 200 years[1] his revolutionary thoughts might have given the people 'ideas'.

'Ye Trewwe Storrie' reveals an idyllic picture of Greenwood life in the romantic thirteenth century, but it unfortunately shows Hood himself to have been something less than the fine, swashbuckling gentleman Errol Flynn would have had us believe.

The following extract from the Rev.

Tuckke's introduction to the work will enable the reader to appreciate the full significance of the verses and why Robin conducted his operations from the Greenwood.

Robbyn Percival Hood was borne on ye 27th daye of Februarye 1241, ye only son of Archibald P. Hood Esq. (of Sherwood Venison Sausages Ltd) and Millicente Thirkettle (attractive brunette housewife) who, it was said, 'had connections with Royaltie'.

Number 7 Holly Wood Gdns. was, however, a humble enough home by all accounts for, important as ye makeinge of sausages was, it was by no means well-paid worke. Wherefore life for ye young Robin and his seventeen sisters was poore but respectable.

At the age of 5 (slightly against his inclinations) ye little lad was obliged to attend Domesday Road Infants School. His greatest pleasure, however, was to help his father in ye shop making ye sausages and sweeping up ye sawdust from the floor at the end of the day. This he could then throw atte people, put discreetly down their bootes – or into ye next day's sausages.

On one occasion, it is recalled, ye lyttel varlet tipped a whole barrell-load over a customer. Unfortunately this manne notte only lacked a sense of humour but was also Ye High Sheriff of Nottingham.

Ye nexte day (still a bitte dustie) this manne returned. To even ye score he burned down Nos. 3 to 17 Holly Wood Gardens, the famous Ethelberta Brewery and the Nag's Head Public House, imprisoned Archibald for 60 years, said very rude things to Robin's sisters (who were at a very impressionable age) and confiscated ye milkman's horse for ye Castle Catsmeatte Company, a rivale organization of which he was the proprietor.

This quite upset ye young lad....

Ye Poemms

Eye shall fynde ye Sheryffe of Nottinghamme
Inn an alley darke and narrowe
And shoot him 'twixt his leg and backe
Wyth my lyttel bowwe and arrowe.

He is a wykedde evill manne
Hys manners are quyte awfulle
So we must seek true justisse out
With methoddes notte quite lawfulle.

He is not kind to aged folk
Who in the winter freeze
He will not give them firewood
So we sell them his trees.

A poore manne may pass bye in peace
To travel is hys righte
A ryche man though mustte pay his taxe
Or else present a fighte.

Our boots are green, our hats are green
Our tights are green as well
And when it rains the dye comes out
We're all as green as hell.

Lyttel John a large manne is
Of Greate and Noble Birthe
And Fryer Tuckke a Goode Manne is
Of even greater gyrthe.

'Tis true I shoot the sheriff's deer
But please don't think me bad
I turns them into sausages
In memory of Dad.

We once packed off our Little John
To go and grab a hostage
The silly fool came back and said
'Oi thort you said a saustidge'.

The Lord, the Knight, the Squire all says
These sausages are nice
While Ladies, dames and serving-girls
Gets everything half-price.

I am a Yeomanne bolde
I like a decent pynte
I love ye barmaid Marrionne
She is a decente bynte.

I dole out farthings to 'ye poore'
They flock from near and far
Not only am I generous
It's good for my P.R.

1. One might well ask why such a long period of time elapsed between the writing of the work and its publication. There are two possible theories: (1) the natural timidity, lack of imagination and entrepreneurial spirit, and general meanness of publishers; and (2) printing hadn't been invented.

33

VII JOLLY GOOD ROBIN HOOD

VIII CANTERS CHAUCERBURY

Dear Mother, Dad, Our Dog and lovely sisters three,
Here's all the news from Holiest Canterbree,
I no longer wish you see to be a punk,
I've changed my plans, I'm going to be a monk.
A pope I'd be if my brain were quicker,
As it is I'll settle for a vicar,
Your lad's become a true religious thinker
He's swallowed it, hook, line, and Holy sinker!
Like you old man I might have joined the army
But discipline would quickly drive me barmy,
A monk in holy orders I shall be,
And study C of E in Canterbree.
I know dear Dad that t'was your desire
That I should be a Doctor or a Squire,
But humble Clergyman's my new vocation,
And Canterbree provides the best location.
'What brings this change of heart?', I fear you say,
'Tis only Fourteen days he's been away,
We packed him off to purify his mind,
Two weeks later, Lo! What do we find?

On pricy package pilgrimage we send,
And now the boy's do-lally; round the bend.'
'Tis true I've been a rascal in my time
But father so were you when in your prime,
How was it that when you were just a lad,
You did the things you did that were so bad?,
Escaping all the various consequences
Of courting maids and dames and serving wenches?
You bragged about your conquests with a laugh
But clobbered me for following your path.
You boasted of your exploits with a wink,
Of your legendary gambling and your drink,
You said that if I ever tell our Mum,
You'd box my ears and kick me up the stairs.
The truth dear Mum and Dad I now must tell,
(And it's not that I am scared of going to hell),
By being friar, monk or holy nun,
And living here you simply get most fun.

G.C.

This superb and moving example of twelfth-century poetry[1], vividly translated into modern English by George Ivor Dunnet, indicates the depth of spiritual devotion of England's most popular saint and martyr, Thos. A. Becket.

Ever since his 'death' at 7.18 pm on 29 December 1170 and his being made a saint by a quarter past eight, people had flocked to Canterbury in their thousands.

'Will no one rid me of this turbulent priest?' shouts Henry II.

'Just as you like, guvnor' say four rather keen knights, and rush off and do it.

'Hang on' says the king, 'I haven't finished yet. I was going to say "for a week or two"'.

But it was too late. The Rev. Thos. Albert Becket lay dead in his second-best night-shirt and a pool of blood on the cold stone floor of Canterbury Cathedral. Mrs Becket was livid.

Thus runs the accepted legend of the martyrdom of Becket. Fortunately, the event did little harm to Henry in particular and Royalty in general as he publicly apologized to all and sundry (and all on Sunday) and did a brief stretch in sackcloth and ashes[2] to prove his point. Becket as we know was instantly made into a top-grade Euromartyr, and as a consequence brought in much valuable foreign currency. For centuries Canterbury was *the* place to visit.

This account of a particularly violent episode in English history has until now been accepted without question. Recent investigation has, however, revealed a series of facts which cast serious doubt upon the true nature of the affair. I present them for your consideration.

1. Henry II was known to be a fine amateur actor.

2. It is a well-known fact that the Rev. Thos. Albert had had enough of being an archbishop by 1170 and had begun to fancy himself as Minister for Tourism.

3. No one actually saw the four knights run him through. And anyway why were they so quick to offer their services? Even in those days it was considered bad form to stab archbishops in the back, especially if they were saying their prayers.

4. Who were these knights, Catchpole, Philtheriche, Frogtarnishe and Loony-braine? If we look closely we find that Thomas Catchpole was the sole proprietor of Catchpole's Cathedral Gifttes; Thomas Philtheriche de Philtheriche just happened to be the largest breeder of palfreys in south-east England; Thomas Frogtarnishe was a major manufacturer of ecclesiastical knick-knacks; and Sir Thomas Loonybraine was none other than the Chairman Elect of Canterbury Chamber of Commerce.

5. Inspection of the Cathedral accounts for the year 1170 has shown that large quantities of red paint were purchased for an unspecified purpose.

The intelligent reader will by now have begun to draw his own conclusions – indeed, the evidence as far as the present writer is concerned is so damning that further investigation may now be considered superfluous. The so-called Murder in the Cathedral was quite simply one of the most brilliant and effective hoaxes of all time: a plot hatched up by King H., the Rev. Thos. Arch. B of C, and the four devil-may-care businessmen. Its instant success exceeded all their wildest dreams and Britain's tourist industry has never looked back since.

As for Thomas, always a man with a bit of 'get up and go', he changed into civvies in the vestry, grew a beard, and became one of the most successful tour operators in the business. A happy by-product from our point of view are his rather amusing travel brochure texts, for which, of course, he adopted the name Geoffrey Chaucer.

Portrait of Henry II taken just after Becket's "Murder"

---

1. Although the poem is signed with the initials G.C., it is by no means certain that it is the work of Geoffrey Chaucer.

2. The medieval name given to Margate Butlin's.

VIII CANTERS CHAUCERBURY

IX MEN OF KENT

REV. John Ball M.P.O.K.

W. Tyler & Co.
Roofing Contractor

Life for the ordinary man and his family was by no means 'all beer and skittles' during the Medieavile Period of English history.[1] Our aristocracy, clergy and military chaps were all either Normans or Norman stooges and therefore more than willing to exploit the good nature of the brave, hard-working, peace-loving, simple-minded Englishman.

However, even green and pleasant Englishmen have their limits, and eventually, in 1381, they decided to call a halt. The exact cause of what has come to be known as The Peasants' Revolt is uncertain. One theory is that one evening a couple of serfs down in Kent (even then the very hub of free thinking) were chatting about this and that following a particularly severe increase in the price of beer when someone said, 'How about a Peasants' Revolt?' 'Steady, lads,' said the landlord, 'we don't want no trouble. I've only just redecorated the Gents.'

Another theory states that it was caused by John Bull, the so-called 'Mad Priest of Kent', who used to slip subversive rhymes into unsuspecting parish magazines. One of his subverses reads:

When Adam delved and Eve span
Who was then a gentleman?

But readers seem to have interpreted this as meaning:

> Just as Adam is about to put his hand in his pocket to pay for his round of drinks in the pub Eve should pretend to faint; then some kind fellow is bound to offer to pay for them himself.

So blame for the Peasants' Revolt can hardly be laid at *his* door.

These are two of the accepted theories regarding the origins of the most important social uprising of the entire Middle Ages which resulted in the untimely death of its stalwart leader Wat Tyler and hundreds of his brave followers.

At no time did they intend harm to Little Richard (the King); they merely sought justice after 315 years of the Feudal System. Perhaps it was the following that suddenly galvanized thousands of good men into marching upon London.

The letters may record a crucial turning-point in English History. They were discovered in the business accounts of a galvanised roofing contractor.

17th December 1380

To: The Steward of His Majesty's Stables

Dear Sir,

With regard to our Invoice No. 4167 dated 10th October I would most respectfully draw your kind attention to the fact that it is now over two months since the work was completed and we would therefore be grateful if you would spare a moment of your valuable time to give the matter your gracious attention. We sincerely trust that the work carried out by us met with your entire satisfaction and would like to say once again how delighted we were to attend to your esteemed order. Should you require further roofing work of this nature we would be only too pleased to provide a quotation at the most competitive rates.

May I take this opportunity to offer you and Mrs Steward the compliments of the forthcoming season.

Assuring you of our best attention at all times, we remain

Yours very sincerely, Wat Tyler (Prop.)

10 January 1381

To: The Steward of His Majesty's Stables

Dear Sir,

With regard to our Invoice No. 4167 of last October and my subsequent letter of December 17th, may I respectfully draw your attention to the fact that we have so far not been in receipt of your kind remittance. We were anticipating that this matter might have been settled prior to the season of goodwill and generosity, so a prompt settlement would oblige.

Thanking you in anticipation,
Yours sincerely, W. Tyler (Prop.)

27th February 1381

To: The Steward of His Majesty's Stables

Sir,

Invoice No. 467, October 10th, Reminder December 17th, Reminder No. 2 January 10th. Please remit.

Yrs etc. W.T.

8th March 1381

To: Walter Tyler & Co. (Roofing Contractors)

Dear Mr Tyler,

Thank you so much for your sundry communications regarding your excellent work on His Majesty's stable block last October. (How time flies, doesn't it?) So sorry for the minor hiccup. This was due to an oversight in the Coffers Department and settlement of your Invoice was inadvertently overlooked. Be assured that this matter will receive our instant attention and the matter is to be put in hand with all speed.

Yours etc. Peveral de Smythe-Smythe

11th March 1381

To: The Steward of His Majesty's Stables

Dear Mr Smythe-Smythe

Thank you for your kind letter of last week regarding payment for our work on the stables. We are glad to hear that the matter is resolved and note that you promise to settle the matter with all speed. We are most grateful that you are giving it your urgent attention.

Thanking you in anticipation,
Yours sincerely, Walter Tyler

16th April 1381

To: The Steward of His Majesty's Stables

Dear Peveral,

I can't believe it, we still have not received your cheque. God knows, it's little enough to charge for all that work. We thought you were giving the matter your 'instant attention'. If we don't get paid soon we're thinking of writing direct to the King and letting him know what kind of inefficient layabouts work for him.

Yrs Tyler

P.S. 'Peveral', indeed, what kind of a bloody silly name is that?

19th April 1381

To: Walter Tyler & Co.

Tyler,

I utterly deplore the tone of your letter of the 16th of April and strongly recommend that you avoid sending such abusive communications again. Such a reaction by you is totally out of all proportion to the piffling little sum involved. We are prepared to overlook your foul manners on this one occasion providing you send a full apology by return of post; when we are in receipt of this we will perhaps consider dealing with the other matter.

Yrs Smythe-Smythe

21st April 1381

To: Steward of His Majesty's Stables

Look here Smythe, if you think I'm going to apologize you're very much mistaken. It might be a 'piffling sum' to you but you were the bumptious skimping little nurk that piffled it. 'Feudal Discount', indeed, what do you think we are, a bloody charity? If we don't get that money by return of post I'll come and get it myself. Tyler.

To: W. Tyler

Just you try. P.

1. This is not borne out by the writings in the Rufus Spratling Chronicle (Chapter VI). However, since the inclusion of this particular piece my colleagues and I are increasingly suspicious as to its authenticity; in fact we now agree that no one but Dame Cecily Thripp I.T.V. would believe a word of it.

IX MEN OF KENT

Catherine of Aragon

Anne Boleyn

Jane Seymour

Anne of Cleves

It has been suggested by rival historians that our glorious and most English of kings, Henry the Eighth, was in fact 'little more than Codpiece and Curtain Material' and only got the job because he was his father's son. Among those who would diminish the stature of one of our greatest monarchs and who ought to know better are, I very much regret to say, a number of scholars of the Oxford and Cambridge variety, thin people who read too many books. (Just where these people get their information from is a mystery to me.) It is as well, therefore, that we remind ourselves of a few of the facts in order to keep things in proportion.

1. Henry did have six wives mostly in consecutive and frequently executive order. They were:

Catherine of Aragon – Spanish Princess and heiress to the Aragon Onion Fortune. Fond of sherry.

Anne Boleyn – bit of a goer. Completely lost her head to him.

Jane Seymour – attractive, brainless, but mother of Edward VI.

Anne of Cleves – nothing whatever like the Holbein portrait.

Catherine Howard – brave, foolish, a bit flighty.

Catherine Parr – decent old stick.

2. Although Henry had only one 'official' son he did naturally have vast numbers of unofficial male offspring. Like any caring father he encouraged them to seek some useful employment as soon as they felt able and to this end he packed them all off to sea at the age of 10. To accommodate them he built a great many fine ships. Henry was therefore known as 'Father of the English Navy', although the sailors were not permitted to call him daddy.[1]

3. Henry was not at all fond of popes: 'Eye don't lyke Eyeties at ye best of tymes but especiallye if they weare girls clothes' he was once heard to say.

4. He was a religious man (a devout glutton) but nevertheless tended to fall out with Cardinals, Monks, etc. He would resolve these little differences either by flattening their monasteries or by removing the offender's head. This latter may seem a little harsh to us but it did at least have the virtue of being effective.

5. Apart from Cardinal-baiting he was fond of other sports too, especially tennis.[2]

6. By far his favourite pastime, however, was eating. For an account of the comestibles consumed by him between 10.45 and 11.02 on the morning of 10 April 1537 we can do little better than refer to 'Ye Kinges Lyttel Booke of Huntinge Elevenses' (published by Piggley & Cochonique in 1539, price 4 groats inc. p. & p.)

Six Large Boyled Hams, Venison Haunches Roasted (4), A demi Butte of goode Malmsey, Six baked Swans, a Boar well stewed, A Butte of Malmsey, A Pottage of Capons Peacocke and Plovers, No Cabbage, Pyes of Quince Sturgeon and ginger pickled Oysters, a Butte of Malmsey, Ye Tablets.

Followed by a note written apparently with the aid of a meat skewer dipped in beef consommé:

Putte bye also a side or three of beef againste such tragedie as my Lord becoming peckish for I have no wyshe to follow mye predecessor to ye choppinge block.

Cook.

Reference is occasionally made to his becoming somewhat portly during his later life. Suffice it to say he weighed little more than 8 Richard IIIs or 3½ Charles IIs (head still attached).

Thus it is clear that Henry was an extremely accomplished man in a great variety of fields (including the Cloth of Gold, of course), but lest this account be considered biased in his favour in any respect, we are prepared to admit one chink in his XL armour. This concerns his legendary musical prowess: he was, we regret to say, not the highly original composer we have been led to believe but about as musical as a tone-deaf lamprey.

This rather shocking discovery was made recently when the following letter was unearthed in the 'odds and sods' box of the Sevenoaks and District Cottage Gardeners' Society. It is reproduced here by kind permission of their Chairperson Dame Cecily Thripp D.D.T., editor of 'Cuttings and Compost Weekly'.

Dear All at No. 4 Cucumber Cotts, Leaves Green, Sevenoaks.

I've been promoted! After only nine years in his mightiness's garden as Veg. 4th class (Special Subject Root Crops) I've been upped to 3rd Class Hedge & Topiary at Hampton Court.

As you know 'tis one of the perquisites of my work to happen upon grand company betimes, well yesterday 'twas no less a person than His Wondrous Majesty Hisself our Great and Glorious King Henry the Great English Eighth. He was a-playing at his 'Tennis'. This Tennis do provide his munificence with much joy and delight for he do love to hit things so. Also, it do provide much opportunity to meet ladies, he do so enjoy their company, especially if they be called Catherine or Anne, and he frequently do entertain such in my potting shed. He do use this shed as a trysting place for all manner of Catherines and Annes and he be not snobbish regarding rank or title I'm pleased to say.

So I am a-clipping my box hedge as happy as a linnet in April when around the corner he do leap like a rutting stag (pardon).

'Gardener!' he do shout as I fall on my face in the John Innes No 2. narrowly avoiding an industrial accident involving the shears.

'Gardener! What tune is that?' (for I was a-whistling our village tune).

Catherine Howard

'Ber Ber B B Begging your Ger Ger Gracious Eeeeeee Enormity's Per P P Pardons...' I stammers. At this he nobly strike me with his tennis batter which do have an immediate and remarkable clearing effect on my brains.

'Whistle that tune again, thou flea-ridden hedgehog' he do roar. 'While your head is still fixed on.'

So I do the best I can - this not being at all easy with his tennis batter resting against my adam's apple.

'Has this tune no words?' he shouts.

'Why yes if it do please your Almighty Corpulence they do go thusly.' I croaks.

'Don't see how I can make this pay,
I ain't catched no moles today,
All the beggars 'ave crept away,
Who'd be a Tuesday Molecatcher'.

'That!' he do say with great expression, 'Was utterly lamentable'.

'Why thank you Your Extreemeness', say I bowing low. He straighten me up smartly with a neat backhand under the chin.

'And what pray is the name of your fine tune?'

'Tuesday Molecatcher's Lament Your Magniloquence' I do say.

'Damn stupid words and a damn stupid title,' he do say 'But a pretty enough tune......Hmmmmmm.' 'And what is your name pray?'

'G Greensleaves Sir, G G G Gilbert Greensleaves'.

With a great shout and a final swipe at my head he do spin away, whether to bed, parliament, dancing, improving the Navy or more of his cardinal baiting I know not but as he do bound along he sing our tune at the top of his dreadful voice. What a Monarch, what a Henry, what a Potenteight.

More news soon,
Your proud son,

Catherine Parr

---

1. The fact is lent extra credence when we remember that Elizabeth I was very fond of sailors but never married one of them as they were likely to be her half-brothers.

2. Yes; Real Tennis with real bats and real balls, what do people keep asking me for? (Author).

X HAMPTON TENNIS COURT

XI READY SIR?

'I Am a Captain Bold, *by F. Drake (Sir)*

(may be sung to a tune not unlike 'Knees Up Mother Brown')

I am a Captain bold, my name is Francis Drake,
The Spaniard only hears my name and in his boots he'll quake.
The ladies they all love me I'm very pleased to say,
And I love all the ladies, but then I sail away.
Ooooooooh!

A sailor's life is rather nice way out across the Main,
Pinch all the gold like a pirate bold and then sail home again.
I love the barmaid Molly, she's famous for her charms,
Works all the day in 'The Lobster Pot' and at night in the 'Fisherman's Arms'.
Ooooooooh!

The Spaniard loves his onions, the frenchmen loves his frogs,
The Eyeties love spaghetti and the Chinese eat their dogs.
Us Englishmen, when we're at home, we like boiled beef and carrots,
But when we're at sea with nothin' for tea we have to eat our parrots.
Ooooooooh!

I love our Queen Elizabeth and I think that she'd love me
If it wasn't for the bloke what laid down his cloak, Sir Walter Ral-eye-ee.
I sailed right round the world in my little wooden ship,
Got a great big kiss from Good Queen Bess and a knighthood for a tip.
Ooooooooh!

Hey ho, Hey Ho me hearties, we're off from Plymouth Hoe,
If it's all the same I'll end this game of bowls afore we go.
You've heard of the Armada, sailed right across from Spain,
Got a fright in the middle of the night and then sailed home again.
Oi!

Lord Effingham

48

This modest little ditty was penned by Drake himself during a force ten gale whilst he was sailing homeward having just beaten the Spanish Armada in 1588. Whilst not precisely in the same class as some of the sonnets attributed to W. Shakespeare (see Chapter XII) it does show a considerable command of language and artistic sensitivity. Though whether he was actually balancing on one leg on top of the mizzen mast playing his concertina having just downed six bottles of rum as legend has it is by no means certain, though it is undoubtedly the work of a man 'in high spirits'.

Drake was by this time the undisputed master seaman of the age, a swashbuckling adventurer afraid of nothing but failure and spiders. He had brought much honour and glory to his country and even more gold and jewellery to his beloved Queen, all at the expense of places like Spain – and quite right too, for Spain was Inquisiting all over the known world and was claiming God-given rights to all the bits that weren't yet known about, like South America, etc.

It was simply no way for a decent, civilized country to behave – or even Spain. And, worse crime still, 'King' Philip had had the infernal cheek to ask our Good Queen Elizabeth to marry him. Her reply by return of post reads:

'You must be joking.'

She was after all perfectly aware of what he was after – and in addition to that he wanted England, no doubt intending to turn us all into 'good' Catholics (possibly with the aid of the odd thumbscrew).

He would have done well to keep his nose out of our affairs and get on with growing onions, but being an ambitious man he sought professional advice.

'Tell you what, Phil' said the Pope one day, 'that woman has got a bit of a thing about sailors – comes from having that dreadful slob Henry as a father, no doubt. Must be fond of boats, too, I should imagine. Why not send her over a bunch of handsome lads in navy-blue in a couple of smart skiffs? She'd like that. Send her a crate

Philip II of Spain

of oranges too: impress her a bit.'

As one might expect from a flash harold like Philip, coming from a flamboyant nation such as the Spanish, the whole thing was completely overdone. Our stalwart lookouts high on the wild cliffs of the Cornish coast peering through the seasonal July mist and rain had no idea that the 800 gigantic galleons glittering with smart uniforms and bristling with armaments were simply a courting gift. The beacons were lit, a fleet assembled, and, as we know, Drake and his men thrashed the living daylights out of them.[1]

Accounts of this glorious defeat often include Sir Francis's famous request that he be allowed to finish his bowls match on Plymouth Hoe before setting about the enemy. This tale, pleasing though it may be, is of course mere legend. He was in fact putting the finishing touches to his Duxon-Drake Patent Cannon Re-Loader, which he was shortly to put to use with such devastating effect and with a little assistance from my Lords Effingham and Blindingham.

Lord Blindingham

---

1. This resulted in a certain loss of Iberian pride and an extra tot of rum all round back at the 'Lobster Pot'.

XI READY SIR?

XII THE WOODEN 'O'

Readers familiar with my previous works will know that the last thing I would ever wish to do is diminish in any way the reputation of one of our great national heroes, so please be assured I am not about to begin now.

The name Shakespeare is without question universally accepted as being that associated with the writing of the greatest theatrical dramas the world has ever produced. In the four hundred years since they were written they have been performed a myriad times, thrilling audiences in every imaginable situation, from the magnificent State theatres of the world's capital cities to the Scout Hall annexe at the back of the Co-op cycle sheds in Chipping Sodbury. Let not the fact that there were actually six William Shakespeares without a single original idea among the lot of them spoil your enjoyment of an otherwise damn good show, say I.

Bill, Billy, Will, William, Big Willy and Little Willy were born in Stratford-upon-Avon[1] in the year 1564, the sons of Mary Arden, 'The Avon Lady', assisted by a Mr W. Shakespeare (senior), an itinerant insurance salesman and first-class amateur pantomime dame. It is believed that they first came across each other at the Stratford-upon-Avon Light Operatic and Hiking Club Xmas Do and it may well have been love at second sight.

The six boys all attended the local Grammar School, where they were outstanding pupils, not so much for their academic abilities but because they all had bald heads and pointed beards at the age of eleven. Their mother continued to take a 'lively interest' in the local Am Drams and we may assume that this is where they acquired their great love of the theatre and Anne 'Hath-a-way'. They married Anne when they were nineteen, she a little older (66) and, as was the custom in those days, they lived in a very old-fashioned house.

The Shakespeare Boys Summer Sing-along was fine for Bumpkinshire audiences but proved far too unsophisticated for the smart London playgoers, so 'something had to be done' when they decided to move down South. There was no shortage of good material around and the names of great playwrights such as Christopher Marlowe, Ben Jonson and Baldrick Fishtonsil spring immediately to mind. One name however stands head and shoulders above the rest and Percivale Pillocke's 'Two Gents of Veruka' and 'Tight as a Dronicus' were justly popular favourites. It was here in London on the South Bank of the Thames that they built their famous Globe Theatre, where one regular visitor was none other than Good Queen Bess herself. (Apparently it was something of a disappointment to Her Majesty to discover that the Shakespeare boys were already married and she consequently took up with a load of sailors and suchlike, poor old soul.)

How is it, then, that so much writing is

ascribed to their name when so little was actually created by them? The answer, indeed the whole premise upon which this 'learned dissertation' is founded, lay undiscovered for nearly four hundred years in an ancient sea captain's trunk recently hauled in with several tons of prime quality halibut. We quote here from just one of the several thousand letters and empty bottles which the trunk contained.

The letter continues in this manner for another several dozen pages but we may consider this to be sufficient for our humble purposes. It is signed Shylock Caliban McBeth (R.N. Retired).

To: Capt. Hezekiah Bracegarnet[2]
c/o Mrs Eliza Goodbody
'Seaview'
The Esplanade
Appledore, N. Devon

Dear Captain Hez

Avast! 'tis I! Your old Armada comrade and shipmate all the way from London Town.

I've found myself a cosy berth ashore at last. I am now, believe it or not, 'Ye Stage Doorkeeper atte ye Globe Theatre' by the River Thames. This is where smart folks come to watch pageants, plays and such. My job is to see the actors in and out of their little hatch round the back, make sure no landlubbers stow away without paying their fare, and generally keep things shipshape. So if I choose I can sail right around the globe every day! Good joke, eh?

The six little gents who captain this rigout are the Shakespeare Brothers – a bit theatrical they may perhaps be, but decent enough and how they do love a good tale. I tells 'em all the old yarns we dreamed up in our days at sea between the decks. Hamlet, Othello, Henry the Fourth Part One, Henry the Fourth Part Two and the one about the storm at sea – they love 'em all. Write 'em all down careful they do as they've terrible bad memories. (Beats me how they remember their words for playing plays.) Like as not at the end of a show they'll walk off with another man's tackle.

'Er, scuse me Mr Shakespeare,' says I, 'But them's Mr Marlowe's notebooks you've got there....' But he'd be gone....

1. The ancient name for STRATFORD-UPON-AVON was Straffa Ponavon.
Straffa (Old English) meaning Sheep-wool or Fleece Ponavon – To Comb, Pull or Yank.
Straffa Ponavon, therefore was a place to yank fleeces. However, more recently it has become better known as a place to fleece Yanks.

2. The Bracegarnets are an old Devonian family and still operate a first-class whelk stall and deckchair hire business in the same vicinity.

XII THE WOODEN 'O'

XIII GOING WEST

It must be said that the good people of America should in no way be criticized for trying to make the most of the pathetic little bit of History that has been allotted to them. Naturally they feel a little aggrieved at the paltry offerings made by so many history books – and who can blame them? Most of us would not be too pleased to be 'discovered' by a third-rate port-swigging dago and settled by a troop of self-righteous miseries dressed in table napkins and ridiculous hats.

One is only too pleased, therefore, to be able to present exciting new evidence which shows that the true Founding Fathers were as fun-loving, relaxed and generous as their counterparts today.

First of all let it be made quite clear that Christopher Columbus did not 'discover' America: it had of course been most happily populated for several millennia by fine folk who enjoyed chasing their buffalos and had a great future in the film business. Columbus called them Red Indians, thus proving that he was not only an incredibly bad navigator but also completely colour blind.

Furthermore, it was only by chance that he got there first as sailing about the world had become extremely popular by this time and we English were particularly good at it – what with our Sir Francis Drake, Albert Ross, Walter Raleigh and, of course, Sir Walter d'Isney.

It was this last hero who captained the famous little ship 'Mayflower' which carried the first colonists to their chosen land. It is perhaps not widely known that there were two ships of that name and this has inevitably led to a certain degree of confusion regarding the true identity of the first settlers. The ships both left Plymouth, Devon, in the autumn of 1620, both weighed about 160 tons, and both carried about the same number of passengers and crew. There, however, the similarity ends, for one party

was quite frankly the most dismal, drab collection of tight-lipped codfish that could be imagined (and in fact they all came home again after two weeks, asking for their money back).

The other much more interesting party, under the command of good Sir Walter had a quite different passenger-list, and I am pleased to be able to quote from it for the first time in print. It was discovered very recently by Captain Ahab R. Bogwicket V.D.Q.S., A.C., V.A.T. 69, brother of the well-known historian of the same name, and required careful deciphering as it was in a severely damaged condition having been used as a beer-mat in the saloon bar of the 'Inebriate Mariner' for as long as anyone could remember. It was painstakingly restored by Captain Bogwicket himself using a secret process which involved, of all things, neat gin, and gradually many of the names on the original passenger-list have been revealed.

As the names were discovered so they were scrupulously checked and double-checked by Bogwicket with great diligence and, it must be said, at considerable personal expense. Much of this work had been completed when, alas, the inevitable happened and funds were exhausted. The British Government did not see fit to finance such a project, important though it was. It seemed only sensible, therefore, to seek aid in the United States itself. This was arranged and generous donations were made – often, it must be admitted, by those hoping that the document would reveal the names of their own ancestors, thus proving that they were amongst the very first settlers in the New World (apart from the Red Indians, of course).

The most exciting fact is that in many cases this proved to be absolutely true, to the great delight of the American benefactors (and to Bogwicket and the landlord of the

'Inebriate Mariner', where most of the research and restoration was carried out.)

We are unable to reproduce the actual document for the time being as restoration is not yet complete. We are, however, delighted to be able to quote from it:

PASSENGERS UPON YE MAYFLOWER, 1620 (Pilgrim Travel Services)

The followinge persones were definitely aboard thyss shippe

Wayne J. Cashlotovitz IV
Laurel Ann Hardy
Mr Charles (Chaplain)
Miss Trixie Wong and her poodles
Uncle Tom Scabin
Henry T. Fordmodel-Black
Barclay Simpson Fine Artz Inc.

It is hardly surprising that since fragments of the list have become available many other like-minded folk from across the Atlantic have expressed a desire to contribute to this valuable work. We are therefore pleased to inform readers that there is still room on the passenger-list for more discoveries. Will those interested kindly send reasonably impeccable references together with an appropriate donation to Bogwicket Enterprises, care of this publisher. (Regret No Credit Cards.)

What, you may ask, became of the seaman hero Walter d'Isney? His grateful passengers wanted to name the whole country after him but, as so often happens with such men, modesty forbade him accepting such an honour. It is, however, still possible to find remote corners known locally as Disneyland.

Artist's Note
A face has been left blank amongst the group-portrait in the foreground. 'Late arrivals' are invited to insert an appropriate photograph.

XIII GOING WEST

XIV FIREWORKERS

The years 1665, 1666 and 1667 dealt a series of terrible blows to Londoners, the like of which they had never experienced before. Three great catastrophes – just like that.

The first began in the Spring of 1665 and was started quite deliberately by rats. This was the plague: red spots, a sneeze and death, in that order. Upon these rats lived fleas, nasty germy little jobs, and the rats, quite understandably wishing to be rid of them, trained them to hop onto any convenient Londoner who happened to be passing. Of course three hundred years later it's a bit difficult to find out who organized it, but since the rats came from abroad the suggestion of an 'inside job' can be discounted.

The same cannot be said, however, for the other two disasters. The Great Fire of 1666 was started by a London architect, while the even more calamitous event of 1667 was actually instigated by the Government itself. This was of course the levy put upon the use of Vestpocket Ale Tankards, or V.A.T. as it was known and it hit the tavern trade like a thunderbolt.

The Great Fire of London was largely the work of one man, an architect with rather grandiose ideas, whose only crime hitherto had been to visit Italy and admire the churches. His name was Christopher Wren and he was not in fact a pyromaniac. (This is not true of Christopher Robin, with whom he should not be confused.)

The fact was that Wren had designed a lot of rather odd-looking churches and had nowhere to build them. They were pitifully un-English in design, being far too florid and Italianate for the average Londoner, who quite rightly prefers a good solid job, with sturdy square towers, thick oak doors, carved pews and pulpits and a bicycle-rack for the curate. Indeed, it is said that when King Charles was shown the plans for a new St Paul's Cathedral he exclaimed, 'Forsooth,

it looks like a monstrous carbuncle on the face of an old friend!' A memorable and poetic phrase.

What is now obvious is that none of these new designs would ever have been carried out if it had not been for the fact that Sir Christopher Wren was a close friend of Ms Nell Gwynne 'actress', who was in turn a close friend of no less a person than King Charles II himself. The complex relationships between these historical figures have been clarified thanks to the recent re-interpretation of the diaries of Mr Samuel Pepys, from which the following extract is taken.

1666
Mon. 27 Aug.
Up betimes to assist Bet ye maid in removing of nits from my periwig. Put on my fine new waistcoat of lavender silk with violet and green velvet bows. To ye office, where chanced upon Sir C. Wren who asketh me (yet again) whether ye Admiralty have any jobs for his architect's practice. No. Haveth Horlicks with ye wife and so to bed.

scarlet trimmings. And so to ye theatre, where Ms. Gwynne performs her new play 'William of Orange' by Max Jaffa. Dined alone with ye wife off eels stewed in Horlicks and so to bed.

Weds. 29 Aug.

Up betimes, three hours louse-hunting with Bet, then put on my lilac and burgundy waistcoats with salmon-pink breeches and plum sash. Ye wife considereth I resemble a dog's dinner. Mette Sir C. Wren at Ye Guy Fawkes Clubbe, who showeth me endless designs for his new churches. "A bit eyetie" I tell him. Dined with him at 'Ye Nimble Rodent Inne' off cold mutton as it is my turn to paye. And so to Vauxhall Pleasure Gardens, where we chance upon Ms N. Gwynne and K. C. II 'conversing' together in an unmarked sedan.

'Allo, allo, allo' sayeth Sir C. 'What haveth we here, then? I wonder what ye Queen will have to say about...'

'Oh all right', sayeth K. C. II 'You can build your confounded churches.'

'And don't forget my gorgeous new theatre, Chrissy darling' sayeth Miss Fruit and Veg. 1642, as sweet as a pickled lemon.

'Thank you, Sire' smarmeth Sir C. 'It will mean making a little space, of course. Would it be all right to have a Great Fire of London, what with demolition being so pricey and all?'

'Go on then, you saucy knave' sayeth K. C. II (for he do so loveth a good joke), 'But give me plenty of warning.'

'Friday all right, Sire?'

'Bit short notice. How about Saturday Night and Sunday Morning?'

'Good idea,' sayeth our Nell. 'We can make a weekend of it. Byeee.' And off goeth the sedan at a rate of knots.

'Who shall we get to light all the fires, Samuel lad?' sayeth Sir C.

'How about ye Apprentice Bakers and

to bed.

Thurs. 30 Aug.

Up betimes to check whether recorder have attracted woodworm during ye night. Put on new silver and burgundy waistcoat with turquoise cuffs and ribbon and so to the Admiralty, where worked most hard and diligent from 11.30 to nearly a quarter after noon. Dined off sucking pig, roasted goose, pies of partridge and hare, baked salmons and sturgeon, followed by junkets, flummeries, possetts and a nice tart. The whole washed down with six bottles of very best french wine as it is Sir. C's turn to pay (and he oweth me a favour).

No Horlicks. Hiccups. And so to bed.

Up betimes during ye night.

Fri. 31 Aug.

Arose with aching of the head and mighty discomfort of ye bowels.

And so to bed.

Sat. 1 Sept.

Up betimes to pack wife off to mother-in-law. Bet assisted me in trying on several new suits and wigs. Have bought a new 'one-piece' wig and hat, so must remember not to doff. Sir C. Wren a bit fidgety at ye theatre. Ms Gwynne out of town with 'a friend', so understudy brought in. Dolly Clackpole – a poor substitute. Dined alone on boiled parsnips, and so to bed.

Sun. 2 Sept.

Up betimes. Strange smell of burning...

Actual Plague Rat

XIV FIREWORKERS

XV GOOD LORD!

What red-blooded Englishman contemplating Nelson's greatest victory at Trafalgar can fail to feel a surge of pride in his heart and an exultation of spirit when he recalls those famous words, that simple but noble phrase that heralded the sudden death of one of our most courageous and best-loved Naval Captains:

'Blimey! They've shot Nelly in the Poop Deck!'

Yes, it was that stalwart jacktar Malachi Harbottle of Portsmouth, mainmast lookout and second rat-catcher aboard the *Victory* who thought he saw the foul blow dealt by a French sniper and shouted those immortal words above the din of battle. (The fact that Nelson was not actually shot in the poop deck but in the left shoulder is quite irrelevant.)

What seemed particularly cowardly to the English was that to all intents and purposes the battle was already over. We had won by the sheer skill and native cunning of two fine men: Nelson himself, of course, with all his wisdom, courage and experience and his famous last message to his men 'England Expects Every Man To Do His Duty', and Malachi Harbottle, who, perched up aloft in the crowsnest, had had the difficult and dangerous job of putting up the signal flags during the course of the battle. Being a brave man he could withstand the difficulty and danger, shrugging off the grapeshot as he courageously made rude gestures at the enemy. What he could not cope with was the spelling and – fortunately as it turned out – he put up the message 'England Expects To Do This Every Munday'.

Admiral Vilenerve, the French commander, had more than a smattering of English (he had been an au-pair boy for six months to George III's hairdresser), and the message

Malachi Harbottle

aiming at Nelson at all, for it would have been a hopeless task for a frenchman to hit such a small target (especially one wearing full protective medals). No, he was actually aiming at one of his own comrades, who had purloined his Dubonnet ration and was making off with it over the side of the ship. It was just an incredible piece of bad luck, then, that poor Nelson was shot at all, and it seems all the more unlikely when we remember that at the time of his death he had so few eyes, arms, legs, etc. of his own that there was very little of the original left to damage.

It is well known that Nelson was of a truly diminutive stature but this did not prevent him from enjoying the company of ladies. One in particular 'took his eye': she was Lady Emma Hamilton, a fine creature whose fabled beauty was matched only by her husband's gullibility. She stood seven

By so many parts of Nelson being made entirely of wood and their topical banter, often at the expense of a certain N. Bona-part, kept both Admirals and sailors amused whenever the fleet was 'in port'.

All these happy memories must have flashed before his eyes as Nelson lay dying. Around him stood his loyal captains and weeping crew. Gunsmoke billowed and cannons roared. Finally he raised his head and said:

'This is like bloody Trafalgar Square. What's that on your face? Looks like a monstrous carbuncle. Please do not kiss me Hardy.'[1]

A particularly violent roar of cannon-fire obliterated all but the last three words of this speech, and as a consequence history books ever since have given a completely incorrect version of the dying words of a fine man.

Nelson's Eggcup

(by kind permission of the Nat. Maritime Museum)

1. Taken from the Harbottle Memoirs, *Malachi Up the Pole* and *Courtmartial Capers*, 2 vols., edited by Capt. A. Ristotle Bogwicket R.N. (dismissed), published by Scurvy & Bilgewater (price 15 guineas o.n.o.).

XV GOOD LORD!

XVI WATERLOO VOLUNTEERS

The Louis constituted a particularly un-pleasant period of history for the poor french and in an effort to prevent yet more they were obliged to have a bit of a Revolution.

It was a case of 'out of the frying pan into the fire', though, I'm afraid, for they got Napoleon Bonaparte, often referred to in french history books as 'Grosse tête sur petites jambes'.

As objective historians we should guard against harbouring any prejudice against this man; suffice it to say that he was a malodorous, scheming little tyke with the manners of a rabid sanglier. Whenever he appeared it invariably meant trouble for frenchmen and human beings alike and in a pathetic effort to look like Horatio Nelson he frequently pretended to have only one arm.

By the time of the Battle of Waterloo[1] he had already bombasted his way around Europe in a vain effort to acquire the attributes of an Emperor, been beaten by Nelson at Trafalgar and by Mother Nature in Russia and exiled to the Isle of Elba.[2] He then crept back to france again. If at that moment he could have found more than half a dozen men in the whole of france with the courage of a dish of snails in garlic he might well have attempted crossing the Channel.[3]

However, Bonaparte had by this time such a high regard for English sea power that he actually considered the utterly futile idea of digging a tunnel *beneath* the English Channel, proving once again that he had more than a touch of insanity about him. He judiciously decided on the poor little Netherlands as a more suitable victim.

'Why are there no tulips in the garden this year? And where is my Edam cheese?'

'Sorry, dearest, but that horrid Boney is messing about in Holland again.'

'Right,' says his Lordship quite angrily, 'That does it, see you later Mrs.'

So he puts on his famous boots, picks up his banjo, leaps on to his horse and jumps aboard the Cross-Channel ferry without even booking.

This brief extract from *Noblesse Obilge*, the great historical novel by Dame Cecily Thripp O.T.T., takes us right to the heart of the matter. For the final confrontation between England and france the stage was now set.

The outcome was pre-ordained and is so well known that no further reference need be made here, for we have no desire to glory over the utterly vanquished. But the exact turning-point, when we may assume that even Boney realized he was a 'gonner', may be of historical interest.

A letter from bandsman Fortinbrass[4] of the Ox. and Bucks. Light Infantry[5] records the decisive moment.

'The Podium'
17 Tripeworks Villas
BUGLETHORPE
Lancs.

Dear Mr Parpjoy

As my music teacher and conductor of the Gas Works Silver Band you will no doubt want to know how I am getting in on King George's Army. I am proud to tell you that I am now a front-rank cornet player and we are currently on a 'European Tour', as it's called.

In fact today it is the Battle of Waterloo and I can hear the roar of cannon a mile or so away. I have just been chatting to one of the locals – a sprout farmer, apparently – a strange little bod in a long grey overcoat six sizes too large and with his hat on sideways. He wanted to know what we were doing.

'Wert her yew dweeng ere,' he garbles through a mouth full of indigestion tablets.

'Practising for tonight's Victory concert, Guvnor,' I tell him.

'Mon Duer! eez eet nert a leetle – owyewsay – premertuer? Zee battel haz honlee jerst begern.'

'Not at all Guvnor, it's only frogs we're fighting 'course we'll win. We always do.'

'Perfidious Albion,' he mutters.

'You hum it and I'll play it Guvnor,' I suggest, 'We're always looking for new numbers.' Then up gallops no less a person than Duke W. Ellington himself.

'Hi man, how's the practice going?' he enquires. 'Don't forget, man, do 'em just as jazzy as you can, man, it don't mean a thing if it ain't got that swing. Say man, is that our new music stand under the dog's blanket?'

'No Duke,' says I, 'It's a sprout farmer with gut's ache.'

'Wow! Crazy man, then put him in the wind section.'

It would have been nice to introduce these two men: on the one hand the greatest soldier and banjo player of his day, whose name would live forever as the inventor of the wellington boot, and on the other, a miserable little crapaud with garlic hiccups. But he had gone. Fast, and in the opposite direction towards france. Perhaps it was all too much for him, couldn't take a joke, you see.

Yours sincerely

Herbert Fortinbrass

P.S. Please thank Mrs Parpjoy for the bedsocks and pontefract cakes – much appreciated, H.

1. A village in what is now called Belgium near Brussels, 'sprout capital of the western world'.

2. 'I cannot tell Madras from my Elba', a phrase signifying a state of personal confusion or inadequacy.

3. The 'courage' of the french soldier is legendary. On one occasion they gallantly persuaded Ms Joan of Arc to dress up as a man and lead the troops. She was eventually burnt as a witch at Rouen (known locally as 'Mother's Rouen' because of the Calvados). On a similar occasion another young lady, already beginning to smoulder, dived into the river to escape. She was later found 'guilty but in Seine'.

4. The collected letters of Herbert Fortinbrass (1798–1899), Letter 29, Vol. 196. General Editor Capt. A. Ristotle-Bogwicket (Adjutant, Mid-Kent Royal Deserters Regiment, Retired Hrt.).

5. 'Ox. and Bucks.' refers to the English counties of Oxfordshire and Buckinghamshire, not to the animals upon which the troops were mounted. US History Scholars please note (could be an exam question).

XVI WATERLOO VOLUNTEERS

XVII STEAMERS

It will have become more than obvious to the diligent reader, whilst studying this collection of essays, that apart from Hadrian's Wall and, to a certain extent, Robin Hood, all the important bits of English History took place in the southern half of England. Just as you'd expect and quite right too, I hear some of you say. But the North of England provided at least two other contributions, which no true record of our glorious past may be permitted to overlook. Their invention and development was to bring respect to our Great Nation throughout the entire civilized world, and, by contrast, even to odd bits of france.

I refer firstly to Yorkshire Pudding.[1] In the momentous days of the Industrial Revolution when Gilbert 'Eh oop lad hast that watter fert t'engine' Chuffleigh with his apprentice James Watt[2] was in the process of developing the very first steam-powered fluctuating reciprocator, where would they have been without a plentiful supply of Yorkshire pudding to clap on the leaks in the pipework? It was only later that it was discovered to be edible, and what seems almost unbelievable to us now is that our ancestors must have been eating roast beef for centuries with no Yorkshire pudding at all. You may well ask 'But how did they sop up the gravy?' Not with mashed potato, because we didn't have any until Sir Walter Raleigh Esq. brought them back as a present for King Edward. The true answer lies in the annals of history (and is probably best left there too).

It was, however, the second major invention, that of Nathan Shufflewick of Scunthorpe, which was to have the most far-reaching consequences. Shufflewick was by profession an engine driver, and at the time of his great discovery had worked on the footplate for almost 68 years. Engineer by day and slag heap warden by night, he still found time to be the local Methodist

preacher, amateur tripe-boiler, and cat poacher at weekends. He was, incidentally, also a much-respected member of the Oddfellows Formation Dance Team during their best-ever 1819-20 season.

The Industrial Revolution was well under way. Men all over the upper half of England were already wearing flat caps and talking like Wilfred Pickles. Thoughtful parents were anxious to secure their children a place in a good coalmine, and it became quite fashionable among the upper classes to attend clog-dancing classes.

While regulating the throttle of his engine, Shufflewick would stand on the footplate and ponder to what further purpose this awesome power could be put. For years he pondered, then at 3.15 p.m. on Tuesday the 18th of March 1818 an idea finally dawned . . .

The invention quickly brought him fame and, as we know, Shufflewick's tea-kettles continued to be used right up to the outbreak of the Second World War. But it was his brother-in-law, Fergus Hotpoint, later Sir Fergus (later still, Lord Typhoo), who was to reap the larger financial reward. Examples of Shufflewick's numerous experiments can be studied at the Grimsby Boiler Museum, where there is a fine collection of 'related artefacts', including the very first arrowroot biscuit-moulds and the prototype of the 'Skegness' Gas Works Cardboard Eight Holer.

Thus was the course of industrial and commercial development set fair for England. It now only remained for our merchants to offload the goods on to unsuspecting foreigners, and for our military chaps to knock India and Ceylon into some sort of shape, and we were poised to conquer the world.

(For a full account see *The Life and Works of Nathan Shufflewick – The Scunthorpe Leonardo,*[3] *Umbrage University Press.*)

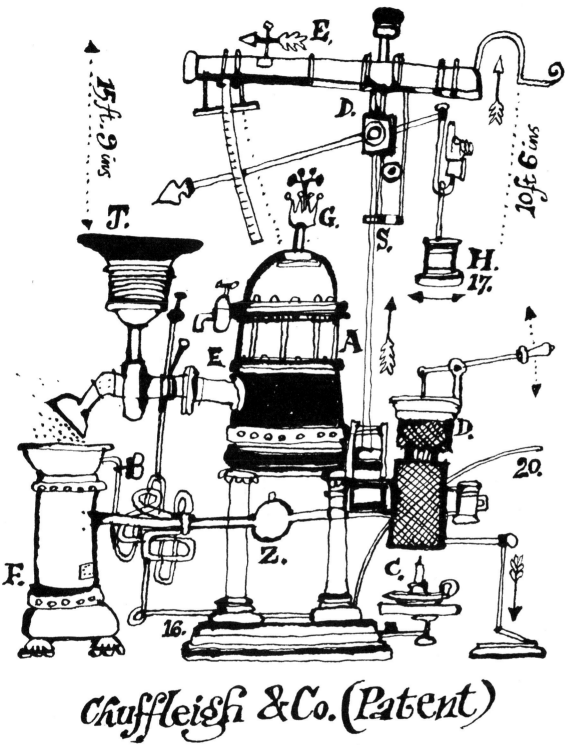

Chuffleigh & Co. (Patent)

Leonard of Finchley
1452–1519

1. It is a curious fact that one single discovery can render world famous (almost overnight, it seems) a hitherto unknown backwater of the globe. Consider, for example Swiss rolls, Chelsea buns and Cheshire cheese, not to mention Dundee cake, Spanish onions, China tea and Jaffa cakes.

2. In addition to Chuffleigh and Watt, other names come naturally to mind; we cannot leave out George Stevenson, for example, nor indeed his sons, Robert and Louis.

3. The 'Leonardo' in the title of the book concerning Shufflewick probably refers to Leonard of Finchley (1452-1519), who adopted the name Leonardo da Vinci (Vinchee) when he took over the family ice-cream business in 1473. He was apparently a keen amateur inventor, and also 'dabbled in oils' in his spare time. His painting of his 'secretary' Liza, dashed off while on holiday in Italy, received a 'highly commended' at the local Arts & Crafts Club Autumn Show.

XVII STEAMERS

XVIII ALBERT ALL

At exactly the same moment as the Industrial Revolution burst upon English History, the Duchess of Kent had a baby in memory of Lord Nelson and his good works and very sensibly decided to call her Victoria.[1]

The poor girl had an extraordinarily dreary and unamusing childhood even though it was in Kensington Palace, where one might expect the odd chuckle, but there was not a moment of jocosity or persiflage to brighten the long days.

Until one day in 1837 when William IV (who was no comedy turn himself) suddenly died.

'Who's going to be monarch now then, Bish?' said the Lord Chamberlain to the Arch. B of C.

'Victoria, of course, she's next in line, and we must be scrupulously fair about these things, you know.'

So they knocked politely on her front door and said, 'Excuse me, Miss, we know you're only eighteen but you've just become Queen of England.'

'Oh Goody Goody,' she exclaimed, highly delighted. 'How long for?'

'Till 1901, Your Majesty, if that's all right by you.'

'Wow! this is going to be amusing,' she cried, 'Let's have a privy council or something.'

'You're the boss now,' said the Lord Chancellor, and they all squashed in.

As can be imagined, with this particular young lady in the royal driving-seat things perked up considerably for England from that moment on.[2]

A year or two later at one of her renowned privy councils she surprised the entire gathering by proclaiming, 'I intend to marry that handsome young man from the Bavarian Christmas Tree Marketing Board. He is so amusing.'

'Heavens above,' said the A B of C. 'Is he a prince?'

'Haven't we got something a bit more English?' questioned Baron Stockmar.

'Nope, nothing that this young lady would poke with a barge pole, anyway. Just thank your lucky stars he's not french.'

'My God, yes,' said the Archbishop gratefully.

Imagine everyone's utter delight[3] and Mama's profound relief when it was discovered that the man of Victoria's dreams was indeed a real live prince.[4] They were in fact so delighted they soon forgot he was German.

Victoria and Albert married in 1840 and it must have been a 'posh do' by all accounts, with jelly, fireworks, conjuring and all the other wonderful things Victoria had missed so much as a girl (including her Albert, of course).

'Do your funny voice, it's so vastly amusing,' she said in the bedroom later.

'Mein Gott vot a Vooman yew arr Missus Kveen. Alvayss choking.'

'Cheeky boy,' she would say.

If everything was so jolly, why do portraits of them always look so stiff and starchy, you may be wondering. The reason is that photography had yet to be invented and our happy couple did not have the time to hold a wide grin for the two or three weeks required by portrait painters. Rest assured that life at 'Chez V & A' was far from dull. They had nine children.

'Mein Gott, Vicki, don't yew sink zat nine Kiddiz iss enuff. Can't yew sink of sumsing else?'

'How about a Great Exhibition, Alby?'

'Off Kiddiz?' he said, clutching his regalia.

'No, don't be soppy, Alby – Science, Discovery, Palm Trees, Inventions, Technical Achievements and that.'

'Verr goot Idea meiner kleiner Pumpernickel, show zee rest of zee World vott our Englant can do, ya!'

And so in 1851 Albert had his Great Exhibition in Hyde Park in a greenhouse known as the Crystal Palace, and a huge success it was too.

The main attractions of the show for the several million visitors were those which Albert had devised, invented or discovered personally.

Some of the more notable amongst them were:

The 'Balmoral' Hip Flask Warmer and Patent Kilt Ventilator

The Telephone (later dubiously attributed to a person called Edison)

Electric Light

The 'Osborne' 625-bladed gent's penknife

A Boxed Set of Home & Hearth Conjuring Tricks

Designs for New Tartans including the McDusseldorf plain grey

Stiff collars

The 'Vicky' 16-hole Crumpet Perforator and Loofah Restorer

The Petrol Engine

An Automatic Corn Law Repealer

An Automatic R. Peel Repealer (at the personal request of Her Majesty)

The Saxe-Coburg-Gothapone (later known simply as the Saxaphone)

The 'Colonel's Chum' Military Boot Stridulator[5]

Tinned Pilchards

Automatic smoking Spats

The Penny-farthing Bicycle

The Three-shillings-and-fourpence-half penny Octacycle

The 'Florence Nightingale' Carbolic Nailbrush Compendium

The Highland Fling Farmer's Friend Manure Dispenser

A Solid Stone Space Vehicle (this never flew from Hyde Park, and was later christened the Albert Memorial)

The Sandringham Steam-driven Eggshell Cracker (as illustrated in the accompanying etching)

Parts of Africa

As can be imagined, after the show, when all the fun was over, there was something of an anticlimax back at the Palace.

'Tell you what, Alby, write some funny books, give us all a bit of a smile.'

'Verr goot idea my kleiner Plumppuddink, I vill.'

So not long after we got the two Charlies, Darwin and Dickens.

The works Albert wrote under the name of Charles Dickens amused Victoria greatly, but the Darwin piece about the monkeys nearly shattered the royal corsets.

'Alby, darling, they're never going to believe this rubbish,' said the Queen, wiping her eyes.

'Chust yew vait und see, Vicki old girl, diss lot vill believe anysink.'

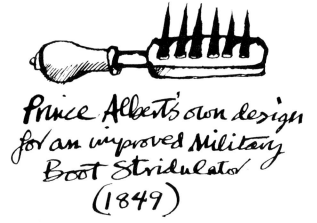

Prince Albert's own design for an improved Military Boot Stridulator (1849)

1. There is a popular misconception that she was found in a Gladstone bag at Victoria railway station. This is not so: she gave her name to the station, not vice versa.

2. All except for 95 per cent of the population who were still poor, overworked and underfed.

3. Everyone except Cecil P. Bodkin (paraffin salesman) of 83a Electricity Villas, Peckham, London, who had hoped to marry her himself.

4. Or so close it made no difference: his name was actually Albert Saxe-Coburg-Gotha and a treble-barrelled name counted as damn near royalty in Germany.

5. A device to roughen the leather soles of brand-new boots and shoes; an article much appreciated even today (unlike the petrol engine, telephone and stiff collars).

It is a matter of regret that not long after this, History becomes rather boring and too much like Real Life to study seriously, so for the time being we'd best put it to one side.

XVIII ALBERT ALL

BIBLIOGRAPHY

Feudal Doodles (Vols. 64–72), Prof. A. Ristotle-Bogwicket, L.N.E.R. (Fungal & Peabody, 1980)

Hezekiah Lampwick: The Skegness Adonis and Vegetarian Longjumper (Filthwright & Gawkley, 1812)

English Social History, G. M. Trevelyan (Longman, 1942)

Keeping Serfs for Fun and Profit, Lady Maria of the Neat Handwriting (Lady Maria Potting Shed Editions)

A New Dictionary of Mid-Shropshire Gravy Browning Labels 1875–1879 (Fibre & Fibre, 1874). 'By far the most exciting book on this subject to date.' (*T.L.S.*)

One Hundred Great Deeds of Gluttony and Pillage, Baron L'Ardydah Piltheyriche de Philtheyrche, a new translation from the original 11th-century french by Dr Herbert Pune, B.O.A.C. (The Lurking Hyena Press, 1955)

Ophthalmic Misadventures of the Mid-Eleventh Century, Dame Cecily Thripp, O.N.O., Rectress (Blatherleigh, Tarbrush & Caloona Ltd., 1960)

Practical Incarceration or How to Practice Serf-control, Every Castle Owner's Guide (Bureau of Norman Wisdom, 1185)

The Rufus Spratling Chronicle – a New Appraisal, R. Spratling of the Rufus Spratling Society (published by the Rufus Spratling Society, 1985)

St Fergus the Unfortunate, Rev. H. 'Pongo' Pigtrinket-Smith, G.W.R. (the life and times of this 8th-century Bedfordshire Tripe Hermit and Brewery Thief in full dramatic detail (The Giggleswick University Press, 1932)

St Blasphemia of the Green Plums, the 12th-Century Tome Martyr, Dame Cecily Thripp, A.G.A.I.N. (out of print)

This is Thanet 'Anit?, Julius Caesar (Tiber & Tiber, 55 BC)

A Treasury of Somerset Manure Smugglers, Des Custing and B. Orkwood (Temsan Udsen Ltd., 1987)

GLOSSARY

Anoraksia Nervosa: fear of looking stupid in garish nylon garments and getting lost on cold wet mountains

Anthropophaggi: cannibals

Arrow: the projectile fired from a bow (wooden arc held taut by a string or thong). It was considered good practice to point the sharp end away from one's person and from the eyes of one's colleagues

Bassoon: a large member of the double reed woodwind family of musical instruments

france: an 'area' of Europe convenient when travelling from Luxembourg to Andorra

french knitting: see 'Tapestry'

Glossary: a special chamber in the Medaeiouville Castle for polishing armour, silver plate, pewter tankards, etc.

Hengist: Eng. Hist. (anag.)

St Riptease, St Arkers and St Ruth: unsuccessful female saints

Saucy (pron. saw see)

Saw: see 'Saw'

Scie (french): saw

Sea Sore: scurvy

Sedan: 'Sedan Sedan Sedan you're rockin' the boat.' A wheel-less conveyance, very cosy for those inside, less comfortable for those manning the handles

SeeSaw (as in 'Comme See Comme Saw')

Tapestry: see 'french knitting'

St Fergus the Unfortunate

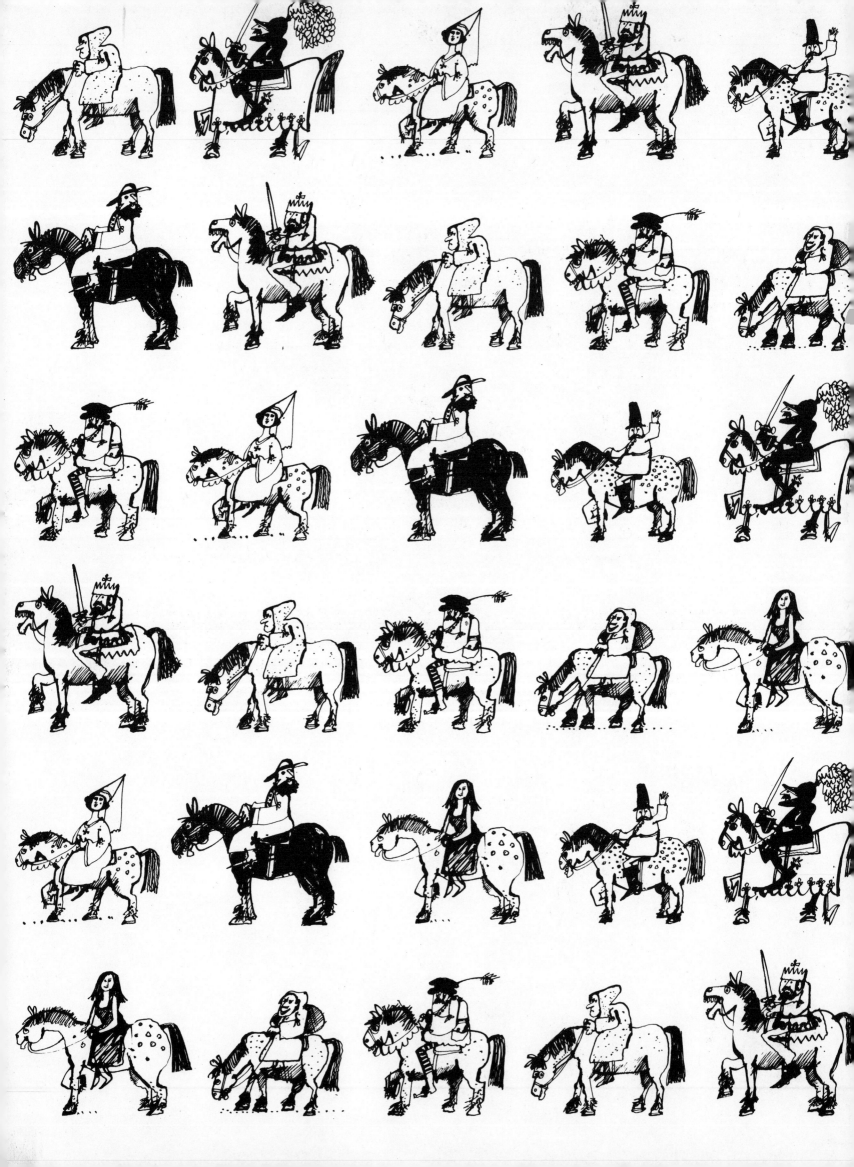